P9-EMB-901

Boris Pasternak
MY SISTER, LIFE
and other poems

Boris Pasternak

# My Sister, Life
### and other poems

Edited and with texts
by Olga Andreyev Carlisle
Color photographs by Inge Morath

A Helen and Kurt Wolff Book
Harcourt Brace Jovanovich
New York and London

*For Vadim and Olga Andreyev*

Many thanks to Paula Schwartz for her excellent
suggestions concerning the rendering of many poems
in this book.

For the cycle *My Sister, Life* we used the Russian
original version, published in 1922 (Berlin,
Petersburg, Moscow).

Printed in Italy

ISBN 0-15-163964-7

First American edition

B C D E

# Contents

Pages in brackets refer to the Russian poems. Titles of the following poems were introduced
by the editor: *My Sister, Life, Is It Not Time for the Birds to Sing, In Everything I Seek to Reach, Tiflis.*

# *Prologue*

BY OLGA ANDREYEV CARLISLE

Boris Pasternak was born in 1890 into a loving, cultivated Moscow family which could be regarded as the epitome of the pre-Revolutionary Russian intelligentsia. His father, Leonid Pasternak, a well-known academic painter, was a close friend and admirer of Leo Tolstoy. His mother was a concert pianist who had given up a promising career in order to devote herself to her children's education. His childhood was extraordinarily happy, protected and stimulating at the same time. Rainer Maria Rilke, Scriabin, Tolstoy, Anton Rubinstein were friends of the Pasternaks. Their presence played a crucial role in the growth of the poet within the young boy.

In his two brilliant autobiographies (1931 and 1957), Pasternak describes the successive emotional experiences, the Kierkegaardian leaps, which marked his emergence as an artist. He was lifted as into space by these spiritual explosions, caused in equal parts by artistic discovery and love.

Pasternak tells us that his sense of himself was born on November 23, 1894, when he was four. One evening, he was awakened by music; he was accustomed to the sound of a piano, but unfamiliar with that of strings. Like "cries for help and news of misfortune," these new sounds frightened him and helped crystallize his sense of memory and his self-awareness.

Much later, in the summer of 1903, came an encounter with the celebrated Russian composer Alexander Scriabin. The composer became the thirteen-year-old boy's idol. With impetuosity and single-mindedness, Pasternak embraced musical composition as a vocation. But this resolve was in turn definitively and rather mysteriously shattered in 1909, during another meeting with Scriabin, whom the young man had not seen in five years. On that day Pasternak gave up music forever, ostensibly because of a sense of technical inadequacy. Scriabin's *fin-de-*

*siècle* artistic egotism and his flamboyance may have played some secret part in the young man's renunciation of music.

Pasternak then immersed himself in philosophy. He remained involved with it until the summer of 1912, when, at the age of twenty-two, he spent a semester at the University of Marburg, in Germany, working under the then famous neo-Kantian philosopher Hermann Cohen. Pasternak was a promising student, and Professor Cohen invited him to stay on in Marburg to continue his studies, thus bestowing on him a great academic honor. But the breakup of a love affair, which occurred toward the end of his semester, had an unexpected effect on the young scholar. It propelled him out of philosophy and into poetry: philosophy was to remain an important element in his life, but from that summer on it was no longer a central concern of his.

Pasternak's parting with philosophy, which is related in his autobiographies and is alluded to in "The Breakup," caused him to view the world with new eyes: ". . . I was surrounded by transformed objects. Something not previously experienced had crept into the essence of reality." All of a sudden "birds, houses and dogs, trees and horses, tulips and people had become more concise and terse than childhood had known them. A fresh laconism of life was revealed to me. It crossed the street, took me by the hand and led me along the sidewalk." The craft of poetry became the young man's life.

Yet another explosion was to rock young Pasternak before he became the man who was to be one of the great poets of his generation. It took place in 1917 and it is of particular interest because it inspired him to write a cycle of poems, *My Sister, Life,* important here. In the exhilarating months that followed the first, bloodless,

Russian Revolution, the February Revolution, Pasternak was seized with a fit of creative fever decisive for his future as a poet. It was triggered by the heady political events of the day, combined with a summertime love affair with a young woman not identified in his autobiographies. Years later, Pasternak was to describe the atmosphere of that period.

*Forty years have passed. From such a distance the voices in the crowd are not reaching us any more, the voices of the people who met day and night in the summer squares, as they had once met in the town squares of Medieval Russia. But even from this distance I still see these meetings, like soundless spectacles or frozen tableaus . . . the simple people opened up their souls and talked about the most important things: how and for what one should live and what means to use to establish the only meaningful and worthwhile existence. The infectious and all-embracing quality of their enthusiasm tore down the barriers between man and nature. During the remarkable summer of 1917, in the interlude between the two revolutions, it appeared as if not only the people participated in the discourse, but together with them also the roads, the trees and the stars, the air, free and unlimited, carried this ardent enthusiasm through thousands of versts and seemed to be a person with a name, possessing clear sight and a soul.*

In *Doctor Zhivago* is found an account of exactly what happened to Pasternak in these summer months:

*After writing some poems which poured out easily, and finding some images which surprised him pleasantly, he [Yuri Zhivago—the poet] saw that the work had taken possession of him; he knew that he was on the threshold of what is known as inspiration. The correlation of forces which determine a work of art seemed to be reversed. The dominant power no longer rested with the human being or the mood he was seeking to express, but with the language, his instrument of expression. Language, the home and container of beauty and meaning, itself begins to think and speak for man, and turns wholly into music, not in the sense of outward and audible sound, but in the sense of the impetuosity and momentum of its inward flow. Then, like the current of a mighty river which polishes stones and turns waterwheels by its very movement, the flowing speech itself creates in its passage, by the force of its own laws, rhyme, meter and rhythm, and a thousand other forms and relationships, even more important and as yet unexplored, unrecognized and unnamed.*

In this new approach to his art, used by Pasternak for the first time in *My Sister, Life* with astounding freshness and power, the ego of the poet seems to disappear: the natural world must not be frightened away as it freely speaks through the poet. This is not far from the frame of mind of a Zen monk "letting a landscape paint itself." Yet of course the person of the artist is all-important: *My Sister, Life* is the expression of an exceptionally harmonious artistic personality, one with a physical and mental sense of equilibrium more often found among painters than writers. Pasternak's innate optimism, his dynamism as a writer, his worshipful love of life in its simplest everyday aspects, are quite unique in the history of poetry. What other poet would have declared to a writers' congress, in Paris in 1935:

*Poetry will always be too simple to serve as a subject matter for discussion at public assemblies; it will remain the organic function of a happy human being, overflowing with all the felicity of language that thrills in a candid and generous heart; and the greater number of happy men, the easier it will be to become an artist.*

Everyday events come to life, irresistibly, in *My Sister, Life.* In it clouds, rain and gardens speak, and so do trains and provincial railway stations. There are no literary clichés, no poetic conventions to be found anywhere. The sonorous, many-sided world asserts itself through an expressive, rhythmic, but completely natural and matter-of-fact tongue. Pasternak's use of colloquialisms may explain why, from the beginning, his writings had the power to irritate a whole class of otherwise sensitive Russian readers. These were the traditionalists who expected literature to be cast in a "literary language." To this day, such people find Pasternak "incomprehensible." In his marvelous introduction to Pasternak's *Selected Works* (Moscow, 1965), Andrei Sinyavsky writes, "In the movement of his poetic language, frequent tonal harmonies arise unintentionally and as if involuntarily. They do not destroy that everyday and conventional intonation which forms the basis of the verse. Just like his metaphors these tonal harmonies are optional and fortuitous because 'the more fortuitous the truer the verses.'" Sinyavsky adds: ". . . having plunged nature into the stream of conversational language, Pasternak dislodged many concepts from the channel of customary associations and provided them with new ones which, although adopted from our immediate surroundings, were unusual because they were not used before in such combinations. The simplest and most natural means of expression then became incomprehensible for an ear accustomed to the notion that in poetry people do not talk the way they do in real life."

Published only in 1922, because of delays imposed by the October upheaval, *My Sister, Life* placed Pasternak among the half-dozen major poets of Russia at that time. He ranked with the greatest, Alexander Blok and Osip Mandelstam.

The nineteen-twenties were a time of extraordinary poetic flowering in Russia. Caught up in the climate of fervor that prevailed there until Stalin all but silenced Russian literature, Pasternak wrote three epic poems on revolutionary themes. They are magnificent. In this book is quoted a fragment of one of them, "1905," dedicated to the first Russian Revolution.

In the thirties and forties, Pasternak was to experience his share of political difficulties, but he was never arrested. It was said that when the name of the poet came up as that of a rebellious writer in need of being disciplined, Stalin declared: "Let this cloud dweller be!" In those years, Pasternak did a number of poetic translations, notably of several plays by Shakespeare and Schiller. He never stopped writing poetry, and the fifties proved a time of heightened inspiration for him. He wrote an epic novel, *Doctor Zhivago,* a saga encompassing the first half of this century in Russia. Its hero, Yuri Zhivago, an autobiographical figure, is a poet as well as a physician. Pasternak's fondest wish was that his novel—an affirmation of Christian faith not particularly anti-Soviet—be published in his country. However, Khrushchev opposed this, thus unwittingly creating one of the great literary sensations of our time. Despairing of seeing his work printed at home, Pasternak authorized an Italian publisher to issue it in the West. In 1958 he was awarded a Nobel Prize for literature, which unleashed a storm in Russia. He was excluded from the Writers Union and reviled at home, while his fame grew in the West and in Russian liberal circles. He was the first Russian writer openly to challenge the Soviet government from within. Today he is worshipped in Russia; his grave in Peredelkino is a national, though unofficial, shrine. He is famous in Russia as a dissenter—second only to Leo Tolstoy.

In the last years of his life, as his work on *Doctor Zhivago* was progressing and he was creating the exquisite crystalline poems that are incorporated in the novel, Pasternak was often vehemently critical of his own early works. He was striving for greater clarity as a poet and now deplored what he considered the sketchiness of his early works. But his voice did not become conventional, lyric as it is in *Doctor Zhivago*. It remained original and immensely fluid. Reading and rereading his poems and his prose, one has the feeling that what the poet had to say, rather than how he said it, was what mattered to him. Formal experiments did not interest him. His words to me in 1960 on this subject echo the words of Yuri Zhivago about inspiration visiting him in his youth. "I have never understood those dreams of a new language, of a completely original form of expression. Because of this dream, much of the work of the twenties was merely stylistic experimentation and has ceased to exist. The most extraordinary discoveries are made when the artist is overwhelmed by what he has to say. In his urgency he uses the old language, and the old language is transformed from within."

Indeed, all of Pasternak's writings have this sense of urgency. Above all, the poet is eager to communicate with his contemporaries. This is why his attitude toward translators—all translators—was benevolent in the extreme. He appreciated the usefulness and humility of their literary role. Having supported his family for years through translations, he understood from inside the nature of a translator's work, its huge limitations and diminutive triumphs assumed for the sake of a goal usually as illusive as it is ill-rewarded. Pasternak's sympathy for translators, which he expressed to me at some length in 1960, encouraged me as I worked on this project. Like Pushkin's, Pasternak's voice is almost impossible to capture in another tongue. Instead, in my adaptations, I have tried to retain the flavor of his uniquely fresh, exhilarating images.

This book was undertaken as much to celebrate Pasternak as a poet as to glorify the visual world under his guidance. A certain number of poems not part of *My Sister, Life* have been included in this selection, although as a leitmotif this cycle, so deeply rooted in the Russian countryside and in Russian literature, was favored. *My Sister, Life* is dedicated to the memory of Lermontov, the most confessional among the Russian romantic poets, "a peal of thunder from the depths of the last century," as Pasternak described him.

Through the inclusion of a variety of poems from different years I have sought to reflect Pasternak's inner world in some detail. Inge Morath's photographs reflect this world visually, from the poet's enthusiasm for revolution in "1905" to the serenity of his later years, so poignantly expressed in "The Wedding." The photographs give the book its form. They determine the sequence of the poems included.

Our project was begun in 1967, when Inge Morath and I were able to travel in Russia together throughout a magnificent apple-and-mushroom-blessed September. In that finest of Russian seasons, we followed in the steps of Pasternak, going to Peredelkino, where the poet had lived, and to other places that inspired him, including Leningrad and Georgia, with which he had fallen in love in the thirties. Back in Connecticut, we studied closely a number of his poems, trying to unlock his images in all their immediacy. It was a long-term collaboration. Fortunately, our interests overlap: Inge Morath is an enthusiastic reader of Russian poetry, while my training as a painter makes me aware of the visual world captured by her camera. Pasternak is a painter's poet, a Post-Impressionist of enormous passion and unity of vision. Painting, his father's profession, occupied an all-important role in his life. Images out of a painter's world abound in *My Sister, Life*. During a thunderstorm:

> *Malice was a wave of rain,*
> *Settling down like charcoal dust*
> *On a sheet of drawing paper.*

There are also images taken from photography:

> *Thunder, tipping its hat,*
> *Took a hundred snapshots,*
> *Blinding us with flashes.*

Among the foundations of his life, which was so closely interlinked with his art as to be inseparable from it, the poet listed, in a letter to Nina Tabidze, the widow of the great Georgian poet, "the example of my father's work as a painter, love of music and Scriabin, two or three chords in my own writings, a night in the Russian countryside, the Revolution, Georgia." These are the foundations we have sought to illuminate through the pictures and the translations in this book.

Gardens, ponds and hedges,
And the whole Universe bubbling
With white roars – this is only
The human heart overflowing.

# СЕСТРА МОЯ – ЖИЗНЬ

### ***

Сестра моя – жизнь и сегодня
            в разливе
Расшиблась весенним дождем обо всех,
Но люди в брелоках высоко брюзгливы
И вежливо жалят, как змеи в овсе.

У старших на это свои есть резоны.
Бесспорно, бесспорно смешон твой резон,
Что в грóзу лиловы глаза и газоны
И пахнет сырой резедой горизонт.

Что в мае, когда поездов расписанье
Камышинской веткой читаешь в пути,
Оно грандиозней святого писанья,
Хотя его сызнова всё перечти.

Что только закат озарит хуторянок,
Толпою теснящихся на полотне,
Я слышу, что это не тот полустанок,
И солнце, садясь, соболезнует мне.

И в третий плеснув, уплывает звоночек
Сплошным извиненьем: жалею, не здесь.
Под шторку несет обгорающей ночью,
И рушится степь со ступенек к звезде.

Мигая, моргая, но спят где-то сладко,
И фата-морганой любимая спит
Тем часом, как сердце,
            плеща по площадкам,
Вагонными дверцами сыплет в степи.

# MY SISTER, LIFE

### ***

My sister, life!
In a flood of spring rain
Life has burst forth!
But bejeweled people living in lairs
Politely sting
Like snakes in the fields.

Older people have their reasons,
And your reason
To them
Is no reason at all,
That eyes and lawns are lilac in the storm,
And skies are smelling of damp mignonette.

That in May in a train compartment
When you read the schedule of the local trains,
It is more impressive
Than the Holy Scripture…
The setting sun
Is my only friend. . . .

In third class,
Apologizing
A bell swims by, a splashing of sound,
"Sorry, not here!"
Under the window shade the sun is smoldering,
And the steppe collapses up to the stars.

Somewhere my beloved
Like Morgan le Fay
Is sleeping sweetly,
While my heart is spilling
Onto the platform,
Hurling carriage doors into the steppe!

# ЗЕРКАЛО

В трюмо испаряется чашка какао,
Качается тюль, и – прямой
Дорожкою в сад, в бурелом и хаос
К качелям бежит трюмо.

Там сосны враскачку воздух саднят
Смолой; там по маете
Очки по траве растерял палисадник,
Там книгу читает Тень.

И к заднему плану, во мрак, за калитку
В степь, в запах сонных лекарств
Струится дорожкой, в сучках и в улитках
Мерцающий жаркий кварц.

Огромный сад тормошится в зале
В трюмо – и не бьет стекла!
Казалось бы, всё коллодий залил,
С комода до шума в стволах.

Зеркальная всё б, казалось, на́хлынь
Непотным льдом облила,
Чтоб сук не горчил и сирень не пахла, –
Гипноза залить не могла.

Несметный мир семенит в месмеризме,
И только ветру связать,
Что ломится в жизнь и ломается
        в призме,
И радо играть в слезах.

Души не взорвать, как селитрой залежь,
Не вырыт, как заступом клад,
Огромный сад тормошится в зале
В трюмо – и не бьет стекла.

И вот, в гипнотической этой отчизне
Ничем мне очей не задуть.
Так после дождя проползают слизни
Глазами статуй в саду.

Шуршит вода по ушам, и, чирикнув,
На цыпочках скачет чиж.
Ты можешь им выпачкать губы черникой,
Их шалостью не опоишь.

Огромный сад тормошится в зале,
Подносит к трюмо кулак,
Бежит на качели, ловит, салит,
Трясет – и не бьет стекла!

24

# THE MIRROR

A cup of cocoa evaporates in the mirror,
The sheer curtain moves,
    and straight as an arrow,
As a path in the garden runs into chaos,
The mirror rushes up to the swing.

The swaying pines fill the air with resin;
A long suffering garden plot
Has lost its glasses in the grass.
There the Shadow reads a book.

Beyond the dark garden gate, shimmering
And mixing twigs and snails,
A path of hot quartz is flowing
Into the medicinal sweetness of the steppe.

Inside the room the enormous garden carouses,
Harasses the mirror,
    yet does not break the glass.
From the bureau to the whispering tree trunks,
The world has drowned in antiseptic amber.

This mirror invasion has settled
Over the world like mistless ice.
It has taken the bitterness out of the branch,
    the scent from the lilac;
Yet the trance persists.

The multifarious world sleepwalks
    with small movements,
And it is only the wind that will link
What breaks into life and what reflects
    in the mirror,
And joyfully plays through tears.

The soul cannot be blasted like coal
    or treasures,
It cannot be dug out from the earth.
Inside the room the enormous garden carouses,
Harasses the mirror, yet does not break
    the glass.

And now in this hypnotic motherland,
I cannot blow out my sight:
In the rain, slugs slither like
The eyes of the statues in the park.

Water rustles past their ears.
The blackbird hops away on tiptoe.
Stain their lips with blueberries—
Your pranks will leave them cold.

Inside the room, the enormous garden
    carouses,
Raises a fist and threatens the mirror.
The garden catches the swing and pounces,
Raises a fist, but does not break the glass.

## ДЕВОЧКА

## THE LITTLE GIRL

Ночевала тучка золотая
На груди утеса великана.

Из сада, с качелей, с бухты-барахты
Вбегает ветка в трюмо!
Огромная, близкая, с каплей смарагда
На кончике кисть прямой.

Сад застлан, пропал за ее беспорядком,
За бьющей в лицо кутерьмой.
Родная, громадная, с сад, а характером –
Сестра! Второе трюмо!

Но вот эту ветку вносят рюмке
И ставят к раме трюмо.
Кто эето, гадает, глаза мне рюмит
Тюремной людской дремой?

A golden cloud spent the night
Against the breast of a giant cliff.
*Lermontov*

Jumping off the seesaw,
The branch rushes from the garden
    into the mirror,
A drop of emerald
On its slender tip.

The garden hides in chaos and movement.
Confusion sets in, it stares one in the face.
The branch is as big as the garden
—Mirror, my beloved twin.

But now the branch is set down by the mirror,
Inside the room in a glass.
It has lost its clear eyes.
Indoors it drowses like a person.

## ГРОЗА МОМЕНТАЛЬНАЯ НАВЕК

А затем прощалось лето
С полустанком. Снявши шапку,
Сто слепящих фотографий
Ночью снял на память гром.

Мерзла кисть сирени. В это
Время он, нарвав охапку
Молний, с поля ими трафил
Озарить управский дом.

И когда по кровле зданья
Разлилась волна злорадства
И, как уголь по рисунку,
Грянул ливень всем плетнем,

Стал мигать обвал сознанья:
Вот, казалось, озарятся
Даже те углы рассудка,
Где теперь светло, как днем.

## A THUNDERSTORM— INSTANTANEOUS FOREVER

Then summer said good-bye to the station.
Thunder, tipping its hat,
Took a hundred snapshots,
Blinding us with flashes.

The lilacs had faded.
From the meadow
Thunder hurled lightning in armfuls.
Now we saw the office building.

On its roof, like heavy fencing,
Malice was a wave of rain,
Settling down like charcoal dust
On a sheet of drawing paper.

Collapsing perceptions blinked.
Boundaries and hidden parts
Of reason, clear as daylight,
Were about to be revealed.

# СВАДЬБА

Пересекши край двора,
Гости на гулянку
В дом невесты до утра
Перешли с тальянкой.

За хозяйскими дверьми
В войлочной обивке
Стихли с часу до семи
Болтовни обрывки.

А зарею, в самый сон,
Только спать и спать бы,
Вновь запел аккордеон,
Уходя со свадьбы.

И рассыпал гармонист
Снова на баяне
Плеск ладоней, блеск монист,
Шум и гам гулянья.

И опять, опять, опять
Говорок частушки
Прямо к спящим на кровать
Ворвался с пирушки.

А одна, как снег бела,
В шуме, свисте, гаме
Снова павой поплыла,
Поводя боками.

Помавая головой
И рукою правой,
В плясовой по мостовой,
Павой, павой, павой.

Вдруг задор и шум игры,
Топот хоровода,
Провалясь в тартарары,
Канули, как в воду.

Просыпался шумный двор.
Деловое эхо
Вмешивалось в разговор
И раскаты смеха.

В необъятность неба, ввысь
Вихрем сизых пятен
Стаей голуби неслись,
Снявшись с голубятен.

Точно их за свадьбой вслед,
Спохватясь спросонья,
С пожеланьем многих лет
Выслали в погоню.

Жизнь ведь тоже только миг,
Только растворенье
Нас самих во всех других
Как бы им в даренье.

Только свадьба, вглубь окон
Рвущаяся снизу,
Только песня, только сон,
Только голубь сизый.

# THE WEDDING

Crossing the yard
To the house of the bride
An accordion player
Came and stayed until dawn. . . .

At dawn when sleep
Is all that matters
He plays again,
Now ready to leave.

He scatters around
The clapping of hands,
The glistening coins.
The dancing begins.

Again the singing
Invades the house.
It ruffles the bed,
The newly-weds are waken.

One, as white as snow,
In the noise and whistling
Like a swan is floating
Moving her hips.

Moving her head
And her hand to the right,
Floating along
Like a swan, like a swan.

Like a stone
Thrown in the water,
Footsteps and music
Vanish at once.

The yard is awake.
A purposeful echo
Muffles the voices
And the peals of laughter....

A blue-grey whirlwind,
The darting doves,
They follow the wedding
Like a flight of good wishes.

Life is an instant,
Life is a gift,
The gift of ourselves
Dissolved into others.

Seen through the window
Life is only a dream,
Life is a wedding,
A blue-grey dove.

# В ЛЕСУ

Луга мутило жаром лиловатым,
В лесу клубился кафедральный мрак.
Что оставалось в мире целовать им?
Он весь был их, как воск на пальцах мяк.

Есть сон такой, – не спишь, а только снится,
Что жаждешь сна; что дремлет человек,
Которому сквозь сон палят ресницы
Два черных солнца, бьющих из-под век.

Текли лучи. Текли жуки с отливом,
Стекло стрекоз сновало по щекам.
Был полон лес мерцаньем кропотливым,
Как под щипцами у часовщика.

Казалось, он уснул под стук цифири,
Меж тем как выше, в терпком янтаре,
Испытаннейшие часы в эфире
Переставляют, сверив по жаре.

Их переводят, сотрясают иглы
И сеют тень, и мают, и сверлят
Мачтовый мрак, который ввысь воздвигло,
В истому дня, на синий циферблат.

Казалось, древность счастья облетает.
Казалось, лес закатом снов объят.
Счастливые часов не наблюдают,
Но те, вдвоем, казалось, только спят.

## IN THE WOODS

The meadows ached with lilac fever;
A cathedral darkness clouded the woods.
What more was left for them to kiss?
It was all theirs, soft as wax to the fingers.

Such is the dream: you do not sleep,
You only dream you thirst for sleep
And some person is dozing, lashes singed
By two black suns which burn his lids.

The sunbeams flow, and iridescent beetles
And dragonflies of glass scurry across
        his cheek.
A busy shimmer fills the woods
Like tweezers probing bright clockworks.

The woods sleep to the ticking of numbers,
While higher up, in bitter amber,
The most elaborate of all the clocks
Is set in accordance with the heat.

Hands and shadows, shaken into movement,
Now penetrate the darkness of the trunks.
They seem to drill and reach the azure dial.
The day's fatigue is rising in the woods.

Old happiness falls like leaves.
The sunset of dreams has seized the woods.
"Happy couples do not watch the clock,"
But these two together only sleep and sleep.

## НЕ ВРЕМЯ-ЛЬ ПТИЦАМ ПЕТЬ

Ты в ветре, веткой пробующем,
Не время-ль птицам петь,
Намокшая воробушком
Сиреневая ветвь!

У капель – тяжесть запонок,
И сад слепит как плес,
Обрызганный, закапанный
Миллионом синих слез.

Моей тоскою выняньчен
И от тебя в шипах,
Он ожил ночью нынешней,
Забормотал, запа́х.

Всю ночь в окошко торкался,
И ставень дребезжал,
Вдруг дух сырой прогорклости
По платью пробежал.

Разбужен чудным перечнем
Тех прозвищ и времен,
Обводит день теперешний
Глазами анемон.

## IS IT NOT TIME
## FOR THE BIRDS TO SING

The wind pokes about
With a branch of wet lilac
Like a tiny wet sparrow:
Is it not time for the birds to sing?

Raindrops heavy as cuff links
And the garden all shiny
Like a pond dotted
With a million blue tears.

Nursed by grief
And still prickly with pain
The garden revives
Filled with whispers and scents.

All through the night
It had knocked at the window.
Suddenly clothes
Smell musty and wet.

Awakened by the magic
Roll call of other days and names,
Today looks out
With eyes like anemones.

СЛОЖА ВЕСЛА

OARS AT REST

Лодка колотится в сонной груди,
Ивы нависли, целуют в ключицы,
В локти, в уключины – о, погоди,
Это ведь может со всякиим случиться!

Этим ведь в песне тешатся все.
Это ведь значит – пепел сиреневый,
Роскошь крошеной ромашки в росе,
Губы и губы на звезды выменивать!

Это ведь значит – обнять небосвод,
Руки сплести вкруг Геракла громадного,
Это ведь значит – века напролет
Ночи на щелканье славок проматывать!

A boat throbs in my sleepy chest.
The willows sway, kissing
Shoulders, elbows, oarlocks.
Wait, this might happen

To anyone! It says so in the song—
The ash-grey lilacs, the splendor
Of daisies crushed in dew,
Lips against lips traded for stars.

This means embracing the firmament,
Embracing Hercules—this means
Whole centuries squandered
On a night filled with the nightingale's song.

Когда случилось петь Дездемоне, –
А жить так мало оставалось, –
Не по любви, своей звезде, она, –
По иве, иве разрыдалась.

Когда случилось петь Дездемоне
И голос завела, крепясь,
Про черный день чернейший демон ей
Псалом плакучих русл припас.

Когда случилось петь Офелии, –
А жить так мало оставалось, –
Всю сушь души взмело и свеяло,
Как в бурю стебли с сеновала.

Когда случилось петь Офелии, –
А горечь слез осточертела, –
С какими канула трофеями?
С охапкой верб и чистотела.

Дав страсти с плеч отлечь, как рубищу,
Входили с сердца замираньем
В бассейн вселенной,
          стан свой любящий
Обдать и оглушить мирами.

When Desdemona was singing
With so little time left for life,
She sang not of love her star,
But of willows, and she wept.

When Desdemona was singing,
Singing about her dark hour,
The darkest demon set for her
A psalm, a weeping riverbed.

When Ophelia was singing
With so little time left for life,
Her parched soul was lifted,
Like stalks of straw in a windstorm.

When Ophelia was singing,
Tired of her bitter dreaming,
What did she carry into nothingness—
An armful of willow sprays and celandine.

Shedding their feelings like old clothes,
Giving up their loving bodies,
They went down into primeval waters.
Their hearts were full of fear.

# ВО ВСЕМ МНЕ ХОЧЕТСЯ ДОЙТИ

Un livre est un grand cimetière où sur la plupart
des tombes on ne peut plus lire les noms effacés.
*Marcel Proust*

Во всем мне хочется дойти
До самой сути.
В работе, в поисках пути,
В сердечной смуте.

До сущности протекших дней,
До их причины,
До оснований, до корней,
До сердцевины.

Всё время схватывая нить
Судеб, событий,
Жить, думать, чувствовать, любить,
Свершать открытья.

О, если бы я только мог
Хотя отчасти,
Я написал бы восемь строк
О свойзтвах страсти.

О беззаконьях, о грехах,
Бегах, погонях,
Нечаянностях впопыхах,
Локтях, ладонях.

Я вывел бы ее закон,
Ее начало,
И повторял ее имен
Инициалы.

Я б разбивал стихи, как сад.
Всей дрожью жилок
Цвели бы липы в них подряд,
Гуськом, в затылок.

В стихи б я внес дыханье роз,
Дыханье мяты,
Луга, осоку, сенокос,
Грозы раскаты.

Так некогда Шопен вложил
Живое чудо
Фольварков, парков, рощ, могил
В свои этюды.

Достигнутого торжества
Игра и мука –
Натянутая тетива
Тугого лука.

## IN EVERYTHING
## I SEEK TO REACH

In everything I seek to reach
The fundamental,
In work
And in love.

I look for the past,
Its causes,
Its roots,
The heart of the matter.

I look for
Life's thread—
Thinking, feeling
And loving.

If only I could,
I would like to write
Eight lines
About the nature of passion.

About pursuit and fleeing,
Unlawful loving,
Chance encounters,
Elbows and palms.

Establishing the laws,
The origins of passion,
I would like to write
Passion's initials.

I would build my poem
Like a garden:
The rows of lindens
Would shimmer and burst into bloom.

In my poem
There would be roses,
Mint, freshly mowed meadows,
The rolling of thunder.

In his études thus
Chopin conjured
Country houses, graves,
Miracles, parks.

Between games and suffering,
An instant of triumph—
The singing
Of a taut bowstring.

ХМЕЛЬ

WILD VINES

Под ракитой, обвитой плющем,
От ненастья мы ищем защиты.
Наши плечи покрыты плащом,
Вкруг тебя мои руки обвиты.

Я ошибся. Кусты этих чащ
Не плющом перевиты, а хмелем.
Ну, так лучше давай этот плащ
В ширину под собою расстелим.

Under trees entwined with ivy
We look for shelter from the rain.
One raincoat covers our shoulders.
My hands are entwined around you.

I am wrong, wild vines, not ivy,
Entwine the branches above us.
Quickly, let us then
Throw the raincoat under us!

52

## Я ВИДЕЛ, ЧЕМ ТИФЛИС

Я видел, чем Тифлис
Удержан по откосам,
Я видел даль и близь
Кругом под абрикосом.

Он был во весь отвес,
Как книга с фронтисписом,
На языке чудес
Кистями слив исписан.

По склонам цвел анис,
И, высясь пирамидой,
Смотрели сверху вниз
Сады горы Давида.

Я видел блеск светца
Меж кадок с олеандром,
И видел ночь: чтеца
За старым фолиантом.

## TIFLIS

I saw how Tiflis
Is attached to its cliff.
Through an apricot tree
I saw it, far and near.

It stood upright
Like a book with a frontispiece.
Magic plum trees
Were painted on its slopes.

Anise trees bloomed.
Like a steep pyramid,
The gardens of David
Looked downward.

I saw the moon
Gleam through the oleanders.
The night was reading
An ancient folio.

ПАМЯТИ ДЕМОНА

IN MEMORY OF THE DEMON*

Приходил по ночам
В синеве ледника от Тамары.
Парой крыл намечал,
Где гудеть, где кончаться кошмару.

Не рыдал, не сплетал
Оголенных, исхлестанных, в шрамах.
Уцелела плита
За оградой грузинского храма.

Как горбунья дурна,
Под решеткою тень не кривлялась.
У лампады зурна,
Чуть дыша, о княжне не справлялась.

Но сверканье рвалось
В волосах, и, как фосфор, трещали.
И не слышал колосс,
Как седеет Кавказ за печалью.

От окна на аршин,
Пробирая шерстинки бурнуса,
Клялся льдами вершин:
Спи, подруга, – лавиной вернуся.

He came at night from Tamara
In the icy-blue light of the glacier.
He marked with his wings
The beginning, the end of the nightmare.

He never wept, nor entwined
His wounded, naked wings.
A gravestone survives
By the wall of a church.

No crippled shadow clawed at the fence.
The lute, barely breathing
In the soft icon light,
Did not whisper about Princess Tamara.

Phosphorescent sparks
Crackled in his hair.
He was never to hear
How the Caucasus turned grey beyond sorrow.

Standing back from the window
He fingered the wool of his cloak.
He swore by the glacier:
"Sleep, beloved, I'll return, a river of ice."

* This is an evocation of the demonic hero of Lermontov's
   "Demon," a romantic poem set in the Caucasus.

# СПАССКОЕ

Незабвенный сентябрь осыпается в Спасском.
Не сегодня ли с дачи съезжать вам пора?
За плетнем перекликнулось эхо с подпаском
И в лесу различило удар топора.

Этой ночью за парком знобило трясину.
Только солнце взошло, и опять – наутек.
Колокольчик не пьет костоломных росинок.
На березах несмытый лиловый отек.

Лес хандрит. И ему захотелось на отдых,
Под снега, в непробудную спячку берлог.
Да и то, меж стволов, в почерневших обводах
Парк зияет в столбцах, как сплошной некролог.

Березняк перестал ли линять и пятнаться,
Водянистую сень потуплять и редеть?
Этот – ропщет еще, и опять вам – пятнадцать
И опять, – о дитя, о, куда нам их деть?

Их так много уже, что не бсё ж – куролесить.
Их – что птиц по кустам, что грибов за межой.
Ими свой кругозор уж случалось завесить,
Их туманом случалось застлать и чужой.

В ночь кончины от тифа сгорающий комик
Слышит гул: гомерический хохот райка.
Нынче в Спасском с дороги бревенчатый домик
Видит, галлюцинируя, та же тоска.

SPASSKOYE

In Spasskoye, memorable September sheds its leaves.
Isn't it time for you to leave the house?
Beyond the fence shepherds' calls are echoing,
And the axe resounds in the woods.

Last night, behind the park, the marshes shivered.
As the sun rose, it disappeared.
The last bluebell drowned in sickly dew,
The birches were full of lilac stains.

The woods were sad, they wanted
To hide under the snow and hibernate.
The park, like a death column,
Could be glimpsed between the tree trunks and the black fence.

The colors of the birchwood were thinning.
They ran, and the woods grumbled:
Here you are, fifteen years old again!
What shall we do with all these years?

There are so many of them,
They are like the birds and the mushrooms.
Once they were their own horizon;
Like a fog they shrouded other distances.

On his deathbed, the typhus-stricken comic
Hears the Homeric laughter of the audience.
From the road in Spasskoye the same huge sadness
Stares, hallucinated, at our house.

## НА РАННИХ ПОЕЗДАХ

\*\*\*

Превозмогая обожанье,
Я наблюдал, боготворя.
Здесь были бабы, слобожане,
Учащиеся, слесаря.

В них не было следов холопства,
Которые кладет нужда,
И новости и неудобства
Они несли, как господа.

Рассевшись кучей, как в повозке,
Во всем разнообразьи поз,
Читали дети и подростки,
Как заведенные, взасос.

Москва встречала нас во мраке,
Переходившем в серебро,
И, покидая свет двоякий,
Мы выходили из метро.

Потомство тискалось к перилам
И обдавало на ходу
Черемуховым свежим мылом
И пряниками на меду.

## EARLY TRAINS

\*\*\*

And, as in church, I humbly watch
Those I revere: old peasant women,
Workers and simple artisans,
Young students from the countryside.

I see no traces of the yoke
Born of unhappiness or want.
They bear the news, the daily trials
Like masters, here to stay.

Fixed in every sort of posture,
Sitting in groups, in quiet knots
The children and the young are still,
Reading, engrossed like wound-up toys.

Now Moscow hails us in a mist
Of darkness turning to bright silver.
We leave the underground
Emerging from this double light.

The young are pressed against the stiles.
They smell of soap and honey cakes.

### 7

Мне в сумерки ты всё – пансионеркою,
Всё – школьницей. Зима. Закат лесничим
В лесу часов. Лежу и жду, чтоб смерклося,
И вот – айда! Аукаемся кличем.

А ночь, а ночь! Да это ж ад, дом ужасов!
Проведай ты, тебя б сюда пригнало!
Она – твой шаг, твой брак, твое замужество,
И тяжелей дознаний трибунала.

Ты помнишь жизнь? Ты помнишь, стаей горлинок
Летели хлопья грудью против гула.
Их вихрь крутил, кутя, валясь прожорливо
С лотков на снег, их до панелей гнуло!

Перебегала ты! Ведь он подсовывал
Ковром под нас салазки и кристаллы!
Ведь жизнь, как кровь, до облака пунцового
Пожаром вьюги озарясь, хлестала!

Движенье помнишь? Помнишь время? Лавочниц?
Палатки? Давку? За разменом денег
Холодных, звонких, – помнишь, помнишь давешних
Колоколов предпраздничных гуденье?

Увы, любовь! Да, это надо высказать!
Чем заменить тебя? Жирами? Бромом?
Как конский глаз, с подушек, жаркий, искоса
Гляжу, страшась бессонницы огромной.

Мне в сумерки ты будто всё с экзамена,
Всё – с выпуска. Чижи, мигрень, учебник.
Но по ночам! Как просят пить, как пламенны
Глаза капсюль и пузырьков лечебных!

For me, at dusk, you are still a schoolgirl.
Winter. The sunset, a woodsman
In the forest of hours. I lie down waiting
For dusk. And now we call out to each other, back and forth.

But the night, the night — it is a torture chamber!
If only you knew — if only something
Would bring you here. Night is your step, your wedding,
Your wedding night, heavier than a court's proceeding!

Do you remember life? The snowflakes
Like doves, their breasts against the howling.
The hungry storm swirled them
And dashed them wildly to the pavement!

You ran across the street. For us the storm was spreading
A magic carpet, sleds and crystals!
Life was a fire, blood gushing
Up to the crimson cloud lashed by the storm.

Do you remember how the crowd was jostling?
The merchants' tents, the icy ringing
Of falling coins? Do you remember
The ringing bells before the holidays, their grumbling?

Alas, my love, all of it must be stated.
What can replace you? What prescription?
Like a horse's eye, from my pillow, feverish,
I look sideways at my own enormous insomnia.

For me, at dusk, you are still a schoolgirl taking exams.
A time of robins, a school recess, textbooks and headaches.
But at night how they clamor, how thirsty
The burning eyes of the medicine bottles!

## БОЛЕЗНЬ III

Может статься так, может иначе,
Но в несчастный некий час
Духовенств душней, черней иночеств
Постигает безумье нас.

Стужа. Ночь в окне, как приличие,
Соблюдает холод льда.
В шубе, в креслах Дух, и мурлычет – и
Всё одно, одно всегда.

И чекан сука, и щека его,
И паркет, и тень кочерги
Отливают сном и раскаяньем
Сутки сплошь грешившей пурги.

Ночь тиха. Ясна и морозна ночь,
Как слепой щенок – молоко,
Всею темью пихт неосознанной
Пьет сиянье звезд частокол.

Будто каплет с пихт. Будто теплятся.
Будто воском ночь заплыла.
Лапой ели на ели слепнет снег,
На дупле – силуэт дупла.

Будто эта тишь, будто эта высь,
Элегизм телеграфной волны –
Ожиданье, сменившее крик: «Отзовись!»
Или эхо другой тишины.

Будто нем он, взгляд этих игл и ветвей,
А другой, в высотах, – тугоух,
И сверканье пути на раскатах – ответ
На взыванье чьего-то ау.

Стужа. Ночь в окне, как приличие,
Соблюдает холод льда.
В шубе, в креслах Дух, и мурлычет – и
Всё одно, одно всегда.

Губы, губы! Он стиснул их до крови,
Он трясется, лицо обхватив.
Вихрь догадок родит в биографе
Этот мертвый, как мел, мотив.

## ILLNESS III

One way or another it can happen:
At some unsuspected, fixed-on moment,
More stifling than clerics droning, night-
Black monks, illness may pounce on you.

Frost. Night at the window, looking,
As is its practice, after the ice thickening.
Wrapped in furs, curled in a roomy armchair,
A spirit purrs away, a pure monotony.

A bough in profile, offering its cheek,
The parquet floor, and the poker's shadow
Out of drowsing and remorse highlight
The daylong, lunatic-raving blizzard.

The night is still, the ice-clear night.
And like a blind whelp lapping milk,
Among fir trees, sunk in their own
Gloom, the pickets lick away at starlight.

Is it the fir trees' thawing gleams,
A candle guttering wildly in the night?
Flicking its paw, the snow blinds fir on fir.
The tree hollows shadow deeper hollows.

This quiet, this sky crouched down,
The telegraph's waves swelling toward elegy,
Did they strain after the cry "Answer!"
Or was it some other silence echoing?

Deafness alone among the twigs and needles,
Deafness among the tongue-tied spheres.
That flicker seems the only answer
In the air to someone's lingering call.

Frost. Night at the window, looking,
As is its practice, after the ice thickening.
Wrapped in furs, curled in a roomy armchair,
A spirit purrs away, a pure monotony.

But his lips! Bitten till they bleed.
He's trembling, his face locked in his hands.
That chalk-white face, those gestures augur
A storm of wonder for the storyteller.

Translated by Theodore Weiss and Olga Carlisle

ЗАМЕСТИТЕЛЬНИЦА

THE REPLACEMENT

Я живу с твоей карточкой, с той,
      что хохочет,
У которой суставы в запястьях хрустят,
Той, что пальцы ломает и бросить
      не хочет,
У которой гостят и гостят и грустят.

Что от треска колод,
      от бравады Ракочи,
От стекляшек в гостиной,
      от стекла и гостей
По пианино в огне
      пробежится и вскочит –
От розеток, костяшек, и роз, и костей.

Чтоб прическу ослабив,
      и чайный и шалый,
Зачаженный бутон заколов за кушак,
Провальсировать к славе, шутя,
      полушалок
Закусивши, как муку, и еле дыша.

Чтобы, комкая корку рукой, мандарина
Холодящие дольки глотать, торопясь
В опоясанный люстрой, позади,
      за гардиной,
Зал, испариной вальса запахший опять.

I live with your picture, the one that laughs,
Whose fingers twist together as they
Lock and bend back till the wrists are breaking,
Whose guests settle sadly to stay and stay.

The one who blazes in flight along the piano
From Rakoczy's bravado, the slap of the cards,
From the ribbons, the roses, the dice,
      the rosettes,
Crystal prisms in the parlor,
      crystal glasses and guests.

Your hair undone, dizzy, a tea rose,
An exhausted tea rose pinned to your belt,
You will dance toward glory effortlessly,
Waltzing and waltzing and holding your breath.

You will swallow the sections of a cool
      tangerine,
Crushing its skin in your hand,
Then rush off to the chandelier-belted
      ballroom,
Where the waltz is again giving off its
      faint scent. . . .

RAZРЫВ

### 3

От тебя все мысли отвлеку
Не в гостях, не за вином, так на небе.
У хозяев, рядом, по звонку
Отопрут кому-нибудь когда-нибудь.

Вырвусь к ним, к бряцанью декабря.
Только дверь — и вот я! Коридор один.
«Вы оттуда? Что там говорят?
Что слыхать? Какие сплетни в городе?»

Ошибается ль еще тоска?
Шепчет ли потом: «Казалось — вылитая».
Приготовясь футов с сорока
Разлететься восклицаньем: «Вы ли это?»

Пощадят ли площади меня?
Ах, когда б вы знали, как тоскуется,
Когда вас раз сто в теченье дня
На ходу на сходствах ловит улица!»

### 5

Заплети этот ливень, как волны,
          холодных локтей
И как лилий, атласных и властных
          беззильем ладоней!
Отбивай, ликованье! На волю!
          Лови их, — ведь в бешеной этой лапте —
Голошенье лесов, захлебнувшихся
          эхом охот в Калидоне,
Где, как лань, обеспамятев,
          гнал Аталанту к поляне Актей,
Где любили бездонной лазурью,
          свистевшей в ушах лошадей.
Целовались заливистым лаем погони
И ласкались раскатами рога и
          треском деревьев, копыт и когтей.
— О, на волю! На волю — как те!

### 6

Разочаровалась? Ты думала — в мире нам
Расстаться за реквиемом лебединым?
В расчете на горе, зрачками расширенными,
В слезах, примеряла их непобедимость?

На мессе б со сводов посыпалась стенопись,
Потрясшись игрой на губах Себастьяна.
Но с нынешней ночи во всем моя ненависть
Растянутость видит, и жаль, что хлыста нет.

Впотьмах, моментально опомнясь,
          без медлящего
Раздумья, решила, всё переиначив,
Что — время. Что самоубийство ей
          не для чего.
Что даже и это есть шаг черепаший.

77

### 3

All my thoughts I now distract from you,
If not at parties, drinking wine, then in heaven!
Surely one day, as the landlord's next-door bell
Is ringing, for someone that door will open.

I'll rush in on them in tinkling December, say,
The door pushed wide — and here I am,
        far as the hall!
"Where've you come from? What's being said?
Tell us the news, the latest scandal from the
        city."

Is all my grief mistaken?
Will it mutter later,
        "She mirrored her exactly,"
As, gathering myself for a leap past forty feet,
I burst out crying, "Is it really you?"

And the public squares, will they spare me?
Ah, if you could only know what pain I feel
When, at least a hundred times a day,
        the streets,
Amazed, confront me with their counterfeits
        of you.

### 5

Like combers twine this cloudburst
        of cold elbows,
Like lilies, silken-stalwart, helpless palms.
Sound the triumph! Break loose! Set to!
        In this wild race
The woods are roaring, choked on the echo
        of Calydonian hunts,
Where Actaeon pursued Atalanta like a doe
        to the clearing,

Where in endless azure, hissing past the horses'
        ears,
They kissed and kissed to the uproarious
        baying of the chase,
Caressed among the shrillest horns
        and crackling trees,
The clattering hoofs and claws.
Like those break loose, break loose,
        rush into the woods!

### 6

So you're disappointed? You think we should
Part with a swan song for requiem,
With a show of sorrow, tears showering
From your eyes dilated, trying their
        victorious power?

As if during mass the frescoes, shaken by
        what's playing
On Johann Sebastian's lips, were to tumble
        from the arches!
From this night on in everything
        my hatred discovers
A dragging on and on that ought to have a whip.

In the dark, instantly, without a thought
My hatred decides that it is time
To plow it all up, that suicide's folly,
Slow, too slow, the speed of a snail.

## 7

Мой друг, мой нежный, о, точь-в-точь как
            ночью, в перелете с Бергена на полюс,
Валящим снегом с ног гагар сносимый
            жаркий пух,
Клянусь, о нежный мой, клянусь,
            я не неволюсь,
Когда я говорю тебе – забудь, усни,
            мой друг.

Когда, как труп затертого до самых труб
            норвежца,
В виденьи зим, не движущих заиндевелых
            мачт,
Ношусь в сполохах глаз твоих шутливым –
            спи, утешься,
До свадьбы заживет, мой друг, угомонись,
            не плачь.

Когда совсем как север вне последних
            поселений,
Украдкой от арктических и неусыпных
            льдин,
Полночным куполом полошущий глаза
            слепых тюленей,
Я говорю – не три их, спи, забудь:
            всё вздор один.

## 8

Мой стол не столь широк,
            чтоб грудью всею
Налечь на борт и локоть завести
За край тоски, за этот перешеек
Сквозь столько верст прорытого прости.

(Сейчас там ночь.) За душный
            свой затылок.
(И спать легли.) Под царства плеч твоих.
(И тушат свет.) Я б утром возвратил их.
Крыльцо б коснулось сонной ветвью их.

Не хлопьями! Руками крой! – Достанет!
О, десять пальцев муки, с бороздой
Крещенских звезд, как знаков опозданья
В пургу на север шедших поездов!

## 9

Рояль дрожащий пену с губ оближет.
Тебя сорвет, подкосит этот бред.
Ты скажешь: – милый! – Нет,
            – вскричу я, – нет!
При музыке?! – Но можно ли быть ближе,

Чем в полутьме, аккорды, как дневник,
Меча в камин комплектами, погодно?
О пониманье дивное, кивни,
Кивни, и изумишься! – ты свободна.

Я не держу. Иди, благотвори.
Ступай к другим. Уже написан Вертер,
А в наши дин и воздух пахнет смертью:
Открыть окно, что жилы отворить.

## 7

My love, my angel, just as in that night
Flying from Bergen to the Pole, the wild geese
Swooping, a snowstorm of warmest down,
    I swear,
O Sweet, my will's not crossed when I urge you,
Dearest, please forget and go to sleep.

When like a Norwegian whaler's wreck,
    to its stock ice-jammed,
A winter's apparition, rigid past its masts, I soar,
Fluttered in your eyes' aurora borealis, sleep,
    don't cry:
All before your wedding day will heal, my dear.

When like the North itself beyond
    the outmost settlements,
Hidden from the Arctic and its ice floe
    wide awake,
Rinsing the eyes of blinded seals
    with midnight's rim,
I say — don't rub your eyes, sleep,
    forget — it's all nonsense.

## 8

My table's not so wide that, pressing my chest
Against its board, I cannot crook my elbow
Round the edge of anguish, those straits
Of countless miles, quarried by "Farewell."

(It's night there now) Ah, to have your cloudy
    hair
(They've gone to sleep) the kingdom
    of your shoulders!

(All lights are out) I'd return them in the
    morning,
And the porch would greet them with
    a nodding branch.

O shield me, not with flakes,
    but with your hands,
Pain's ten sufficient fingers, the spikes
Of winter stars, like the placards of delay
Posted on trains northbound into blizzards!

## 9

The trembling piano licks foam from its lips.
This delirium, tossing, will strike you down.
You murmur, "Dearest!" "No!" I cry back.
    "Never
In the midst of music!" And yet how could we
    be closer

Than in the twilight here, the score like a diary,
Page after page, year after year,
    tossed on the fire.
O wondrous memories that, luring us still,
Astonish the spirit! But you are free.

I shan't keep you. Go on. Give yourself
    to others.
Leave at once. Werther's already had his day.
But now the air itself reeks death:
Opening a window is like opening a vein.

Translated by Theodore Weiss and Olga Carlisle

## ЗИМНЯЯ НОЧЬ

Мело, мело по всей земле
Во все пределы.
Свеча горела на столе,
Свеча горела.

Как летом роем мошкара
Летит на пламя,
Слетались хлопья со двора
К оконной раме.

Метель лепила на стекле
Кружки и стрелы.
Свеча горела на столе,
Свеча горела.

На озаренный потолок
Ложились тени,
Скрещенья рук, скрещенья ног,
Судьбы скрещенья.

И падали два башмачка
Со стуком на пол.
И воск слезами с ночника
На платье капал.

И всё терялось в снежной мгле
Седой и белой.
Свеча горела на столе,
Свеча горела.

На свечку дуло из угла,
И жар соблазна
Вздымал, как ангел, два крыла
Крестообразно.

Мело весь месяц в феврале,
И то и дело
Свеча горела на столе,
Свеча горела.

The snow swept through the land
To the ends of the earth.
On the table a candle,
A candle was burning.

Like moths in the summer
Attracted by flames,
Crowding and rushing
—snowflakes at the window.

The blizzard had drawn
White circles and arrows.
On the table a candle,
A candle was burning.

Shadows softly mingling
On the luminous ceiling,
Arms and legs intertwining,
Destinies crossing.

Two tiny slippers
Fell to the floor,
And the candle was weeping
Wax tears on her dress.

All swirled in the darkness,
Snowy and grey.
On the table a candle,
A candle was burning.

The candle was almost
Put out by a draft.
The heat of temptation
Raised its wings like an angel.

A February blizzard,
Lasting a month.
On the table a candle,
A candle was burning.

Ужасный! – Капнет и вслушается:
Всё он ли один на свете
Мнет ветку в окне, как кружевце,
Или есть свидетель.

Но давится внятно от тягости
Отеков – земля ноздревая,
И слышно: далеко, как в августе,
Полуночь в полях назревает.

Ни звука. И нет соглядатаев.
В пустынности удостоверясь,
Берется за старое – скатывается
По кровле, за желоб и через.

К губам поднесу и прислушаюсь:
Всё я ли один на свете,
Готовый навзрыд при случае,
Или есть свидетель.

Но тишь. И листок не шелохнется.
Ни признака зги, кроме жутких
Глотков и плескания в шлепанцах,
И вздохов и слев в промежутке.

The terrible one, it drips and listens,
Is it still alone in this world?
It crushes the lacy branch at the window,
Or – is there a witness?

But the earth, like a sponge,
Is aware of its weight; it is choking,
And one hears, in the distance
As in August, midnight ripening.

Not a sound, no observers, no witnesses.
Secure of its own aloneness,
It starts again, rolling
Down the roof and beyond the gutter.

I will put it to my lips,
And listen. Am I still alone in this world?
Ready to burst into tears,
Or – is there a witness?

Silence, not a branch moving,
Darkness, only the sinister
Sobs and the splashing of slippers,
Between the sighs and the weeping.

# АННЕ АХМАТОВОЙ

Мне кажется, я подберу слова,
Похожие на вашу первозданность.
А ошибусь, – мне это трын-трава,
Я всё равно с ошибкой не расстанусь.

Я слышу мокрых кровель говорок,
Торцовых плит заглохшие эклоги.
Какой-то город, явный с первых строк,
Растет и отдается в каждом слоге.

Кругом весна, но за город нельзя.
Еще строга заказчица скупая.
Глаза шитьем за лампою слезя,
Горит заря, спины не разгибая.

Вдыхая дали ладожскую гладь,
Спешит к воде, смиряя сил упадок.
С таких гулянок ничего не взять.
Каналы пахнут затхлостью укладок.

По ним ныряет, как пустой орех,
Горячий ветер и колышет веки
Ветвей и звезд, и фонарей, и вех,
И с моста вдаль глядящей белошвейки.

Бывает глаз по-разному остер,
По-разному бывает образ точен.
Но самой страшной крепости раствор –
Ночная даль под взглядом белой ночи.

Таким я вижу облик ваш и взгляд.
Он мне внушен не тем столбом из соли,
Которым вы пять лет тому назад
Испуг оглядки к рифме прикололи.

Но, исходив из ваших первых книг,
Где крепли прозы пристальной крупицы,
Он и во всех, как искры проводник,
Событья былью заставляет биться.

## FOR ANNA AKHMATOVA

It seems to me that I am choosing
Words that reflect your elemental power.
But if I err, it does not matter,
I must persist in my mistakes.

I hear the small talk of the wet roofs,
The muffled eclogues on the wooden pavement.
A certain city is clear from the beginning,
It grows and echoes in every sound.

Spring is here, but there is no leaving the city;
The demanding customer is sharp.
Eyes full of tears from sewing by lamplight,
Sunset, like an unbending seamstress, lingers on.

The seamstress yearns for the reaches
      of Ladoga,
And hastens to the water's edge,
But this is useless.
The canals smell like musty closets.

The hot wind, a hollow walnut,
Dives and stings the seamstress' eyelids,
The eyelids of stars, branches and milestones.
Standing on the bridge she gazes.

Like eyes, poetic images vary in sharpness.
Now the white night fades into the distance.
The strongest mortar
Is the white night, gazing upon darkness.

This is how I see you, your vision.
It is not inspired by that pillar of salt
Conjured by you five years ago,
Lot's wife, the fear of glancing back.

Your vision springs from your first books,
Full of prosaic, glistening particles.
It's everywhere, a live conductor
Turning events into throbbing reality.

Барабанную дробь
Заглушают сигналы чугунки.
Гром позорных телег –
Громыхание первых платформ.
Крепостная Россия
Выходит
С короткой приструнки
На пустырь
И зовется
Россиею после реформ.

Это – народовольцы,
Перовская,
Первое марта,
Нигилисты в поддевках,
Застенки,
Студенты в пенсне.
Повесть наших отцов,
Точно повесть
Из века Стюартов,
Отдаленней, чем Пушкин,
И видится
Точно во сне.

Да и ближе нельзя:
Двадцатипятилетье – в подпольи.
Клад – в земле.
На земле –
Обездушенный калейдоскоп.
Чтобы клад откопать,
Мы глаза
Напрягаем до боли.
Покорясь его воле,
Спускаемся сами в подкоп.

Тут бывал Достоевский.
Затворницы ж эти,
Не чаяв,
Что у них,
Что ни обыск,
То вывоз реликвий в музей,
Шли на казнь
И на то,
Чтоб красу их подпольщик Нечаев
Скрыл в земле,
Утаил
От времен и врагов и друзей.

Это было вчера,
И, родись мы лет на тридцать раньше,
Подойди со двора,
В керосиновой мгле фонарей,
Средь мерцанья реторт
Мы нашли бы,
Что те лаборантши –
Наши матери
Или
Приятельницы матерей.

1905
(A fragment)

The drums' throbbing is drowned in the roar of the railroad;
The scraping of wheels on the executioner's cart
Drowns in the sharp harangue from the speaker's platform:
Russia, the Land of Serfs, acclaims its reforms.

By the prison gate, this is the Will of the People —
Bespectacled students, Nihilists clad for work.
The tales of our fathers sound like reigns of the Stuarts,
Further away than Pushkin, the figures of dreams.

Here Dostoevsky came, and the faithful women.
Who thought that each arrest would yield us a relic?
Rather, they met their deaths assuming oblivion:
Nechaev,* underground dweller, buried them deep.

Ah, were it yesterday, thirty years past, and, strolling,
I'd light that doorway with my flickering kerosene lamp,
The young girls bent in the dark there, warrior-chemists
With their bombs, would be my mother and her friends.


* The story of this shadowy revolutionary-adventurer
inspired Dostoevsky's *The Possessed*.

ГАМЛЕТ

HAMLET

Гул затих. Я вышел на подмостки.
Прислонясь к дверному козяку,
Я ловлю в далеком отголоске
Что случится на моем веку.

На меня наставлен сумрак ночи
Тысячью биноклей на оси.
Если только можно, авва отче,
Чашу эту мимо пронеси.

Я люблю твой замысел упрямый
И играть согласен эту роль.
Но сейчас идет другая драма,
И на этот раз меня уволь.

Но продуман распорядок действий,
И неотвратим конец пути.
Я, один, всё тонет в фарисействе.
Жизнь прожить – не поле перейти.

The roaring stops. I walk onstage.
I lean against the doorframe
And try to catch, like Hamlet,
The echo of all that will happen in my time.

The night stares darkly,
And a thousand opera glasses,
On their handles, stare. I implore you,
Abba, Father, take this cup away!

I respect your stubborn planning.
I agree to act this part.
But another play is now unfolding,
Take me off the stage tonight.

The sequences have been arranged,
It is the end, the road is running out.
I am alone among the Pharisees.
To live a life is not to cross a field.

# Conversations with Pasternak

In the winter of 1960, shortly before Pasternak's death, I went to Moscow and was able to meet and to interview the poet. I have described these meetings with him in *Voices in the Snow*.

I had messages and small presents to take to him from my parents and from other admirers. But how to get in touch with him? I soon learned that Pasternak had no phone. I dismissed the thought of writing a note, because I feared that he might have some sort of standard rejection form for requests to visit him. My only choice, then, was to go directly to his house, but it took great effort to bring myself to call unannounced on a man so famous. I was, moreover, afraid that Pasternak in his later years would not live up to my image of him, suggested by his poems—lyric, impulsive, above all, youthful.

My parents had mentioned that prior to being awarded the Nobel Prize, Pasternak had held open house on Sundays. (This, as a matter of fact, seems to be a tradition among Russian writers, and it extends to Russians abroad.) On my third Sunday in Moscow I decided to call on Pasternak at his home in Peredelkino. It was a radiant day, and the center of Moscow looked like the dream of the winter city. The streets were full of sightseers—out-of-town families bundled in peasantlike fashion walking toward the Kremlin with faces full of expectation. Their festive air was accentuated by the fresh mimosa many carried, sometimes only a single spray. On Sundays in wintertime large shipments of mimosa come to Moscow. Russians buy it to present to each other or perhaps simply to carry around, as if to mark the solemnity of the day.

I decided to take a taxi to Peredelkino, although I knew of an electric train which went from the Kiev railroad station, near the outskirts of Moscow. I was suddenly in a great hurry to get there.

The taxi driver, a youngish man with the anonymous air of taxi drivers everywhere, assured me that he knew the way to Peredelkino, which was about thirty kilometers out of town on the Kiev highway. He seemed to find it completely natural that I should want to drive out to the country on that lovely sunny day.

But the driver's claim to knowledge of the way turned out to be a boast, and we soon got lost. There were a few discrete road signs, but they failed to direct us to our destination, and so we began stopping to ask for directions. Everyone was friendly and willing to help, but nobody seemed to know of Peredelkino, and we became more and more lost. We rode for a long time on an unpaved frozen road in the middle of endless white fields.

Finally we entered a village which was in complete contrast to the massive apartment projects growing on the outskirts of Moscow. There were low, ancient-looking log cottages bordering a straight snowy main street. A horse-drawn sled went by; women in kerchiefs were grouped near a small wooden church. It turned out this was a settlement very close to Peredelkino called Pavlenko. A five-minute drive on a small winding road through dense evergreen trees and I was in front of Pasternak's house. I suddenly recognized it on my right, a brown building, with bay windows overlooking the road. I had seen photographs of it in magazines.

Peredelkino is a loosely settled little town, hospitable-looking and cheerful in the sunny midday. I had been told that it was inhabited by writers and artists, but most of Peredelkino looked like a settlement of small artisans and peasants; there is nothing "arty" about it, although it is one of the most important writers' colonies near Moscow. The village has a large rest home for writers and journalists, which is run by the Soviet Writers Union. Kornei Chukovsky lives in the town, in a cozy frame house, where he entertains his family and close friends on Sundays. Konstantin Fedine has a house next door to Pasternak's. He is now the first secretary of the Writers Union—a post long occupied by Alexander Fadeyev, who also lived in Peredelkino, until his death in 1956. A long time ago, Isaac Babel was arrested here. The house where he lived can be seen from Pasternak's house, lost in the snow beyond a deep ravine.

Pasternak's house is on a gently curving country road which leads down the hill to a brook. On that sunny afternoon the hill was full of children on skis and sleds. Across the road there is a large fenced field. It is a communal field, cultivated in the good season; now, in winter, it was a vast white expanse dominated by a little cemetery—like a bit of background from a Chagall painting. The tombs are surrounded by wooden fences painted bright blue, and the crosses are planted at odd angles. There were brilliant pink and red paper flowers on the

The house of Boris Pasternak in Peredelkino

tombs, half buried in snow. It is a cheerful cemetery. Beyond it, in the distance, children skated on a frozen pond, small, swift figures gliding in wide circles.

The veranda of Pasternak's house gives it a superficial resemblance to an American house of forty years ago, but the firs against which it stands mark it as Russian. They grow very close to each other and give the feeling of deep forest, although there are only small groves of them around Peredelkino. Those trees, behind low scalloped fences, lend a fairy-tale air to the lanes of the settlement. I was to find out that while visiting in Peredelkino one is always taken for walks on the snowy lanes. Walks are an established part of life in Russia—like drinking tea.

I paid the driver and with great trepidation pushed open the gate in the fence separating the garden from the road. I walked up to the dark house. On the small veranda at the side of the house there was a door with a withered half-torn note pinned on it saying: "I am working now. I cannot receive anybody. Please go away." After a moment's hesitation, I chose to disregard it, mostly because it looked so old, but also because of the little packages in my hands. I knocked, and almost immediately the door was opened—by Pasternak himself.

He was wearing an astrakhan hat. He was strikingly handsome. With his high cheekbones and dark eyes and fur hat, he looked like someone out of a Russian folk tale. He was in perfect keeping with the tall fir trees and the wooden houses and the horse-drawn sleds. After the increasing anxiety of the trip, I suddenly wondered why I had ever doubted that I would see Pasternak.

I introduced myself as Olga Vadimovna Andreyeva. Andreyev is a fairly common Russian name, however, and it took him a minute to realize that I was Vadim Leonidovich's daughter and that I had come from abroad to visit him. He greeted me with great warmth, taking my hand in both his hands, and asking about my mother's health and my father's writing, and when I was last in Paris. I felt he was looking closely into my face in search of family resemblances. He said he was just going out to pay some calls. Had I been a minute later, I would have missed him. He asked me to walk part of the way with him — as far as his first stop, the Writers' Club.

One walks into Pasternak's house through the kitchen, to be greeted by a tiny, smiling, middle-aged cook, who helps to brush the snow off one's clothes with a little wicker broom. Here, one may take off one's overshoes and overcoat. Then comes the dining room, with a bay window where geraniums grow. On the walls hang charcoal and sanguine studies by Leonid Pasternak, the writer's father, who was a well-known and talented academic Russian painter. There are life studies and portraits. One recognizes Tolstoy, Gorky, Scriabin, Rachmaninoff. There are sketches of Boris Pasternak and his brother and sisters as adolescents, of ladies in big hats with veils. It's very much the world of Pasternak's early reminiscences and of his poems about adolescent love. It echoes the world of *War and Peace*.

While Pasternak was getting ready to go, I had a chance to look around the room. From the moment I stepped inside the house, I was struck by its resemblance to Leo Tolstoy's house in Moscow, which I had visited a few days before. It had the same atmosphere of both austerity and hospitality. Pasternak's house retained what must have been characteristic of a Russian nineteenth-century intellectual's home. Both houses are furnished with comfortable but utterly unpretentious old furniture; both look like ideal settings for a studious life or for informal entertaining. Needless to say, Tolstoy's house, although it was extremely simple for the times, is a great deal vaster and more elaborate than Pasternak's; but the lack of concern for elegance or display is the same. In Pasternak's own words, it was a house in which "simplicity argued with comfort."

Ten or fifteen minutes later, Pasternak was ready to leave. We stepped out into the sunlight and walked through the evergreen grove behind the house in rather deep snow, which quickly managed to get into my citified Swiss-made boots. The sunlight had started to turn yellowish with the advancing afternoon, but it was still warm.

Soon we were on a country road where the snow was packed and much more comfortable to walk on, although it had treacherous icy patches. Pasternak was quite tall and walked with long lanky steps. On particularly perilous spots — deep snow or snow slippery as ice — he would take my arm. Otherwise he gave all his attention to the conversation. He seemed to love walking. We took what was obviously a

*The pond in Peredelkino, where Pasternak liked to walk, and which he described in some of his poems*

roundabout path to the Writers' Club. The stroll lasted for about forty minutes, during which I felt an increasing friendliness on Pasternak's part. He plunged right away into an absorbing discussion of the art of translating, but he digressed from time to time to ask about the political and literary situation in France and America. He said that he rarely read papers, "except when I sharpen my pencil and happen to glance over the sheet of newspaper into which I collect the shavings. This is how I learned last fall that there was a near revolution against De Gaulle in Algeria, and that Soustelle was ousted. Soustelle was ousted," he repeated with satisfaction, emphasizing both his approval of De Gaulle's decision and the similarity of the words in Russian. Actually, he seemed well informed about literary life abroad, and American literature interested him particularly.

From the first moment, I was charmed and

impressed by how much Pasternak's speech was like his poetry—full of alliterations and unusual images. He related words to each other musically, without, however, sounding affected or sacrificing the exact meaning. His word sense was so inventive and acute that one felt his conversation was but the continuation of a poem—waves of words and images following each other in a crescendo.

Later in our acquaintance, I remarked to him on the musical quality of his speech. "In writing as in speaking," he said, "the music of the word is never just a matter of sound. It does not result from the harmony of vowels and consonants. It results from the relation between the speech and its meaning. And meaning—content—must always come first."

Pasternak appeared young and in good health. It was hard to believe that I was walking next to a man of seventy. There was something a little strange and forbidding in this youthfulness, as if something—was it art?—had mixed itself with the very substance of the man to preserve it. Even his movements were completely youthful—the gestures of the hands, the manner in which he threw his head back. His friend the poetess Marina Tsvetayeva once wrote: "Pasternak looks at the same time like an Arab and like his horse." And indeed, with his dark complexion and archaic features, Pasternak did have something of an Arabic face. At certain times he seemed suddenly to become aware of the impact of his own extraordinary looks, of his whole personality. Then he seemed to withdraw for an instant, half closing his slanted brown eyes, turning his head away, vaguely reminiscent of a horse balking.

In Moscow, I had been told that Pasternak was a man in love with his own image—but then, I had been told so many different things about Pasternak in the past few weeks. Pasternak was a living legend—a hero to some; to others, a man who had sold out to the enemies of Russia. It was his character Doctor Zhivago who seemed most controversial; many young people arbitrarily identified Pasternak the man with the fictional Yuri Zhivago.

In any event, I found that there was no truth to the charge that Pasternak was egocentric. On the contrary, he seemed intensely aware of the world around him and reacted to every change of mood in people near him. It is hard to imagine a more perceptive conversationalist. He grasped the most elusive thought at once. The conversation lost all heaviness. Although he had seen my parents only a few times in his life, he remembered everything about them, their background, their tastes, their opinions. He recalled with surprising exactness some of my father's poems which he had liked. I soon discovered that it was difficult to get him to talk about himself, which I had hoped he would do.

As we walked in the winter sunshine, I told Pasternak what attention and admiration Doctor Zhivago had aroused in the West and particularly in the United States, despite the fact that the translation into English does not do justice to his book.

"Yes," he said, "I am aware of this interest and I am immensely happy and proud of it. I get an enormous amount of mail from abroad about my work. In fact, it is quite a burden at times, all those inquiries that I have to answer, but then, it is indispensable to keep up relations across boundaries. As for the translators of *Doctor Zhivago,* do not blame them too much. It's not their fault. Like translators everywhere, they tend to reproduce the literal sense rather than the tone of what is said: in translating, it is the tone that is important. Actually, the only challenging translations are those of classics. It is rarely rewarding to translate modern works, although it might be easy. You said you were a painter. Well, translation is very much like copying paintings. Imagine yourself copying a Malevich. Wouldn't it be boring? And that is precisely what I have to do with the Czech Surrealist poet Nezval. He is not really bad, but all this writing of the twenties has aged terribly. The translation which I have promised to finish and my own correspondence take much too much of my time.

"As you can imagine, some of the letters I get about *Doctor Zhivago* are quite absurd. Recently somebody writing about *Doctor Zhivago* in France was inquiring about the plan of the novel—I guess it baffles the French sense of order. But how silly, for the plan of the novel is outlined by the poems accompanying it. This is partly why I chose to publish them alongside the novel. They are there also to give the novel more body, more richness. For the same reason, I used religious symbolism, to give warmth to the book. Now some critics have become so wrapped up in those symbols— which are put in the book the way stoves go into a house, to warm it up—that they would like me to commit myself and climb into the stove. . . .

"Scholars interpret my novel in theological terms. Nothing is further removed from my understanding of the world. One must live and write restlessly, with the help of the new reserves that life offers. I am weary of this notion of faithfulness to a point of view at all cost. Life around us is ever-changing, and I believe that one should try to change one's slant accordingly—at least once every ten years," he added jokingly. "The great heroic devotion to one point of view is alien to me—it's a lack of humility. Mayakovsky killed himself because his pride would not be reconciled with something new happening within himself—or around him."

We had reached a long, low wooden fence, and Pasternak stopped at the gate. Our walk had already made him late. I said good-bye with regret. There were so many things that I still wanted to ask him. Pasternak showed me the way to the railroad station, very close by, downhill behind the little cemetery. A little electric train took me into Moscow in less than an hour.

My subsequent visits with Pasternak merge in my memory into one long conversation. Although he declined to give me a formal interview—"For this, you must come back when I am less busy, next fall perhaps"—he was interested in the questions I outlined to him. Except for meals, we were alone, and there were no interruptions. Each time as I was about to leave, Pasternak kissed my hand in the old-fashioned Russian manner, and asked me to come back the following Sunday, so that for a brief period—three or four weeks—there was a pattern to my visits.

I remember coming to Pasternak's house from the railroad station at dusk by taking a shortcut near the cemetery. Suddenly the wind grew very strong; there was the beginning of a snowstorm. I could see snow flying in great round waves in the distant lights along the railroad station. It grew dark very quickly; the wind was so strong that I had difficulty walking. I knew this to be fairly customary Russian winter weather, but it was my first actual blizzard in Russia. It evoked Pasternak's early poems, and the snowstorms of *Doctor Zhivago.* It was strange to step into Pasternak's house a few moments later and hear his elliptic sentences, so much like his verse.

I had arrived too late to attend the midafternoon dinner. Pasternak's family had retired, and the house seemed deserted. Pasternak insisted that I have something to eat, and the cook brought some venison and vodka into the dining room. It was only about four o'clock, but the room was dark and warm, shut off from the world, with only the sound of snow and wind outside. Pasternak sat across the table from me.

Although I was hungry and the food delicious, I found myself regretting the fact that I had to eat instead of giving my full attention to what Pasternak was saying about my grandfather. Pasternak had recently reread some of his stories and liked them a great deal. "They bear the stamp of those remarkable years in Russia, the nineteen-hundreds. Those years are now receding in our memory and yet they loom in the mind like great mountains seen in the distance, enormous. Andreyev was under a Nietzschean spell; he took from Nietzsche his taste for excesses. So did Scriabin. Nietzsche satisfied the Russians' longing for the extreme, the absolute, their taste for the grandiose. Music, writing—men had to have this enormous scope before they acquired specificity, became themselves."

Pasternak told me about a piece he had recently written for a German magazine on the theme "What is man?" "How old-fashioned Nietzsche seems, he who was the most important thinker in the days of my youth! What enormous influence—on Wagner, on Gorky . . . Gorky was impregnated with his ideas. Actually, Nietzsche's principal function was to be the transmitter of the bad taste of his period. How quickly his aura faded! It is Kierkegaard, barely known in those years, who was destined to influence our own epoch. I would like to know the works of Berdyaev better; he is in the same line of thought, I believe—truly a writer of our time."

It grew quite dark in the dining room, and we moved to a little sitting room on the same floor, where a light was on. Pasternak brought me tangerines for dessert. I ate them with a strange feeling of something already experienced: tangerines often appear in Pasternak's work—in the beginning of *Doctor Zhivago,* in early poems. They seem to stand for a sort of ritual thirst-quenching. And then there was another vivid evocation of a Pasternak poem—like the snowstorm that blew outside—an open grand piano, black and enormous, filling up most of the room:

*… could we be closer*
*Than in the twilight here, the score like a diary,*
*Page after page, year after year, tossed on the fire.\**

On the walls, as in the dining room, there were simply framed sketches by Leonid Pasternak. Half-familiar faces of writers of the turn of the century looked upon us.

I had heard from people who had seen him while he was working on *Doctor Zhivago* that Pasternak rejected most of his early verse as too tentative and dated. I had difficulty believing it. There is a classical perfection to *Themes and Variations* and *My Sister, Life,* as experimental as they were in the nineteen-twenties. I found that writers and poets in Russia knew them by heart and would recite them with fervor. Often one could detect the influence of Pasternak in the verse of young poets. Mayakovsky and Pasternak, each in his own manner, are the very symbol of the years of the Revolution. Then, art and revolutionary ideas seemed inseparable. It was enough to let oneself be carried by the wave of overwhelming events and ideas. There were fewer heartbreaking choices to make, and I sensed a longing for those years on the part of many young Russians. Was it true that Pasternak rejected those early works?

In Pasternak's reply there was a note of slight irritation. It might have been because he didn't like to be admired solely for those poems, or perhaps he unconsciously resented the thought that he could never write anything that could equal them. Or was it the more general weariness of the artist dissatisfied with past achievements, concerned only with immediate artistic tasks? Eventually, as I felt Pasternak's detachment from *Doctor Zhivago* at the expense of his new play, I tended to believe the latter.

"I have the feeling of an immense debt toward my contemporaries. I wrote *Doctor Zhivago* in an attempt to repay it. This feeling of debt was overpowering as I slowly progressed with the novel. After so many years of writing only lyric poetry or translating, it seemed to me that it was my duty to make a statement about our epoch — about those years, remote and yet looming so closely over us. Time was pressing. I wanted to record the past and to honor the beautiful and refined aspects of the Russia of those years. There will be no return of those days, or those of our fathers and forefathers, but in the great blossoming of the future their values will revive, I know. In the meantime, I have tried to describe them. I don't know whether my novel is fully successful, but then, with all its faults, I feel that it has more value than those early poems. It is richer, more humane than the works of my youth. Those poems were like rapid sketches — just compare them with the works of our elders. Dostoevsky and Tolstoy were not just novelists, Blok not just a poet. The voices of those writers sounded like thunder because they had something to say.

* From "The Breakup," *Themes and Variations,* 1918.

As against the facile artists of the twenties, take my father for an example. How much effort went into one of his paintings! Our success in the twenties was partly due to chance. My generation found itself naturally at the focal point of history. Our works were dictated by the times. They lack universality: now they have aged. Moreover, I believe that it is no longer possible for lyric poetry to express the immensity of our experience. Life has grown too cumbersome, too complicated. We have acquired values which are best expressed in prose. I have tried to express them through my novel, I have them in mind as I write my play."

"Among your contemporaries' writings," I asked him, "whose do you think have best endured?"

"You know how I feel about Mayakovsky. I have told it at great length in my autobiography *Safe Conduct*. I am indifferent to most of his later works, with the exception of his last unfinished poem, 'At the Top of My Voice.' The falling apart of form, the poverty of thought, the unevenness which is characteristic of poetry in the late twenties are alien to me. But there are exceptions. I love all of Essenin, who captures so well the smell of Russian earth. I place Tsvetayeva highest; she was a formed poet from her very beginning. In an age of affectations she had her own voice—human, classical. She was a woman with a man's soul. Her struggle with everyday life was what gave her strength. She strived for and reached perfect clarity. She is a greater poet than Akhmatova, whose simplicity and lyricism I have always admired. Tsvetay-

eva's death was one of the great sadnesses of my life."

"What about Andrei Bely, who was so influential in those years?"

"Bely was too hermetic, too limited. His scope is comparable to that of chamber music—never greater. If he had really suffered, he might have written the major work of which he was capable. But he never came into contact with real life. . . . Perhaps this fascination with new forms is the fate of writers like Bely who die young. I have never understood those dreams of a new language, of a completely original form of expression. Because of this dream, much of the work of the twenties was merely stylistic experimentation, and has ceased to exist. The most extraordinary discoveries are made when the artist is overwhelmed by what he has to say. In his urgency he uses then the old language, and the old language is transformed from within. Even in those years one felt a little sorry for Bely because he was so cut off from the immediate, which alone could have helped his genius to blossom."

"What about today's young poets?" I asked. "I am impressed by the extent that poetry seems a part of everyday life for Russians. Large printings of works by young poets are amazing to a Westerner. Poetry in Russia seems very alive."

"Well, perhaps not as much as you think. It is fairly limited to a group of intellectuals. And today's poetry is often rather ordinary. It is like the pattern on a wallpaper, pleasant enough but without a real *raison d'être*. Of course some

*The church in Peredelkino*

young people show talent. Yevtushenko, for example. However, as I was saying earlier, I believe that prose is today's medium, elaborate, rich prose like that of Faulkner. Today's work must re-create whole segments of life. This is what I am trying to do in my new play. But everyday life has grown very complicated for me. It must be so anywhere for a well-known writer, but I am unprepared for this role. I don't like a life deprived of secrecy and quiet. It seems to me that in my youth work was an integral part of life, and illuminated everything else in it. Now it is something I have to fight for. All those demands by scholars, editors, readers cannot be ignored, but together with the translations they devour my time. . . . You must tell people abroad who are interested in me that this is my only serious problem—this terrible lack of time."

My last visit with Pasternak was longer than

the others. He had asked me to come early, in order to have a talk before a midafternoon dinner with the family. It was again sunny. I arrived at his house shortly before he returned from his morning stroll. As I was shown into his study, the house echoed with cheerful voices. Somewhere in the back of it, members of his family were assembled.

Pasternak's study was a large, rather bare room on the second floor. Like the rest of the house, it had little furniture — a large desk near the bay window, a couple of chairs, a sofa. The light coming from the window looking over the large snowy field was brilliant. Pinned on the light-grey wooden walls was a multitude of art postcards. When he came in, Pasternak explained to me that those were all sent to him by readers, mostly from abroad. Many were reproductions of religious scenes — medieval nativities, St. George killing the dragon, Mary Magdalene. . . . They were related to *Doctor Zhivago*'s themes.

After his walk, Pasternak looked especially well. He was wearing a collegiate-looking navy-blue blazer and was in a good mood. He sat at the desk by the window. I remember vividly feeling happy; Pasternak looked so gay and the sun through the window was almost springlike. As we sat there, I wished our talk could be prolonged somehow. But the three or four hours I spent across the desk from Pasternak vanished like an instant. When we came down to the dining room, the family was already seated around the large table. "Don't they look like an Impressionist painting," said Pasternak, "with the geraniums in the background and this late-afternoon light? There is a painting by Guillaumin just like this. . . ."

Everybody stood up as Pasternak came down. Besides Madame Pasternak — Zinaida Nicolaevna — Pasternak's brother Alexander was there with his wife, a grey-haired lady of great dignity. Pasternak presented his youngest son, Lenya, a handsome boy, dark, eighteen or twenty years old, with quite a strong resemblance to Zinaida Nicolaevna. He was a student in physics at Moscow University. Professor Enrich Nihaus was also a guest. He is a famous Chopin authority and teaches at the Moscow Conservatory; Madame Pasternak had once been married to him. Sviatoslav Richter is one of his most famous pupils. He was quite elderly and charming, with an old-fashioned white mustache.

I was seated to the right of Pasternak. Madame Pasternak was at his left. The table was covered with a white linen tablecloth embroidered with red cross-stitch. The silverware and china were simple. There was a vase with mimosa in the middle, and bowls of fruit — oranges and tangerines. The hors d'œuvres — caviar, marinated herring, pickles, macédoine of vegetables — were already on the table. Guests passed them to each other, as Pasternak poured out vodka. Then kvass was served, a homemade fermented beer usually drunk in the country. Because of fermentation, the kvass corks would sometimes shoot into the night and wake everybody up — just like a pistol shot, said Madame Pasternak. After the hors d'œuvres, the little cook served a succulent stew of game.

At first the conversation centered around

Hemingway. He was one of the most widely read authors in Moscow, and a new collection of his writings had just been published. Madame Pasternak and the ladies at the table remarked that they found Hemingway monotonous—all those endless drinks, with little else happening to the heroes! Pasternak, who had fallen silent during much of this discussion, took up Hemingway's defense:

"The greatness of a writer has nothing to do with subject matter itself, only with how much the subject matter touches the author. This results in a density of style, and it is this density that counts. Through Hemingway's style you feel matter, iron, wood. . . ." He was punctuating his words with his hands, pressing them against the wood of the table. "I admire Hemingway but I prefer what I know of Faulkner. *Light in August* is a marvelous book. The character of the little pregnant woman is unforgettable. As she walks from Alabama to Tennessee, something of the immensity of the South of the United States, of its essence, is captured for us who have never been there."

Later the conversation turned to music, and Professor Nihaus and Pasternak began talking about Chopin. Pasternak said how much he loved Chopin. "A good example of what I was saying—Chopin used the old Mozartian language to say something completely new—the form was reborn from within. Nonetheless I am afraid that Chopin is considered a little old-fashioned in the West. I gave a piece on Chopin to Stephen Spender, which was not published." I told him how much André Gide loved to play Chopin. Pasternak didn't know this and was delighted to hear it. This somehow reminded him of Proust, whom he was reading for the first time.

"Now that I am coming to the end of *Remembrance of Things Past,* I am struck by how it echoes some of the ideas that absorbed us in 1910. I put them into a lecture about 'Symbolism and Immortality,' which I gave on the day before Leo Tolstoy died. This must have been just about the time when Proust was first thinking of his book. The text of my lecture has long been lost, but among many other things, it said that although the artist will die, the happiness of living which he has experienced is immortal. If it is captured in a personal and yet universal form it can actually be relived by others through his work.

"I have always liked French literature," he said. "Since the war I feel that French writing has acquired a new accent, less rhetoric. Camus's death is a great loss for all of us." Earlier, I had told Pasternak of Camus's tragic end, which took place just before I arrived in Moscow. It was not printed in the Russian press. Camus has not been published in Russia. "In spite of differences of themes, French literature is now much closer to us. Only where French writers commit themselves to political causes are they particularly unattractive. Either they are cliquish and opportunistic or with their French sense of logic they feel they have to carry out their beliefs to their conclusion. They fancy they must be absolutists like Robespierre or Saint-Just. I mostly dislike those writers who make a career out of being Communists."

Tea and cognac were served at the end of the

meal. Pasternak suddenly looked tired and became silent. As always during my visit in Russia, I was asked innumerable questions about the West—about its cultural life and our everyday existence. Lights were turned on as we drank our tea at leisure. I looked at my watch to discover that it was long past six o'clock. I had to go. I too suddenly felt tired and I had yet to pack my bags. I was leaving Moscow very early the next day.

Pasternak walked me to the door through the kitchen. We said good-bye outside on the little porch in the blue snowy evening. I was terribly sad at the thought of not returning to Peredelkino. Pasternak took my hand in his and held it for an instant, urging me to come back very soon. He asked me once again to tell his friends abroad that he was well, that he remembered them even though he hadn't time to answer their letters. I had already walked down the porch and into the dark path when he called me back. I was happy to have an excuse to turn back, to have a last glimpse of Pasternak standing bareheaded in his blue blazer under the door light.

"Please," he called, "don't take personally what I have said about not answering letters. Do write to me, in any language you prefer. I will answer you."

*Pasternak's tomb in Peredelkino*

# CAPTIONS

For the most part, Inge Morath's color photographs do not require explanatory captions; they speak for themselves and for the poems with which they are presented. In some cases, however, specific buildings and locations need to be identified.

| | |
|---|---|
| Page 24 | Summer Garden (Letnii Sad), Leningrad. Laid out by Leblond in 1712, it contains 75 marble sculptures from Venice of the early 18th century. |
| Pages 32/33 | Country wedding in Moldavia. |
| Page 46 | Vegetable garden behind Peter Ilych Tchaikovsky's house in Klin, north of Moscow. |
| Page 52 | Tbilisi market, Georgia. |
| Page 55 | 11th-century Church of the Holy Cross on Georgia Military Highway, near Mishket. |
| Page 57 | Window in cottage where Pushkin spent his honeymoon, in Pushkin, formerly Tsarskoye Selo, north of Leningrad. |
| Page 61 | *Isba* (wooden house) in Central Russia. |
| Page 63 | Part of the old Kremlin wall, Moscow. |
| Pages 64/65 | Red Square, Moscow, with the Cathedral of St. Basil (Vasili Blazhenni Cathedral), begun by Ivan the Terrible in 1554, consecrated in 1557, completed in 1679. |
| Page 67 | View toward Red Square, Moscow— in the center, the Historical Museum; in the background, the towers of St. Basil's and the square structure over Lenin's tomb. |
| Page 76 | Cupolas on top of the Czarina's "Golden Apartment," inside the Kremlin, on Cathedral Square, Moscow. |
| Page 92 | Mikhailovskoye. Pushkin, who was exiled by Czar Alexander I to this estate, belonging to his great-grandfather Hannibal, wrote several works here, among them *Eugene Onegin*. |
| Pages 94/95 | View of the Neva and the Palace Quay from the roof of the Fortress of Peter and Paul, Leningrad. |
| Page 97 | Gardens of the Ostankino Palace, Moscow. |
| Pages 98/99 | Palace Square (Dvortzovaya Square), with the crescent-shaped buildings of the General Staff quarters and the Alexander Column. The square played an important part in the revolutionary history of Leningrad. |
| Page 101 | Façade of St. Isaac's Cathedral, the largest church in Leningrad, silhouetted against the evening sky. |
| Page 105 | Portrait of Boris Pasternak (*Archive of Olga Andreyev Carlisle*). |